THE

FAMILY

BUDGET

WORKBOOK

GAINING CONTROL OF YOUR PERSONAL FINANCES

LARRY BURKETT

NORTHFIELD® PUBLISHING

CONTENTS

INTRODUCTION

To many people, the word *budgeting* has a bad ring. Why? Because they see budgeting as a punishment plan. Unfortunately, often this has been the case with many families attempting to correct in one day financial problems that have been developing for several years.

It does not have to be so; a budget is simply a financial plan for the home. What is proposed in this workbook is a simple, workable plan for home money management; one that brings the financial area under control and relieves the burdens of worry, frustration, and anxiety. It maximizes family finances so that we are more effective financially. From this foundation the budget becomes a tool for good communications in an area normally characterized by conflict.

SECTION 1

GETTING STARTED

GETTING STARTED

THE GOAL—LIVING WITHIN OUR MEANS
WHAT DOES THIS MEAN?

It means to spend no more than we make on a monthly basis. Ideally that means to live on a cash basis and not use credit or borrowed money to provide normal living expenses. It also means the self-discipline to control spending and keep needs, wants, and desires in their proper relationship.

NEEDS	WANTS	DESIRES
These are the purchases necessary to provide your basic requirements such as food, clothing, home, medical coverage, and others.	Wants involve choices about the quality of goods to be used. Dress clothes vs. work clothes, steak vs. hamburger, a new car vs. a used car.	These are choices that can be made only out of surplus funds after all other obligations have been met.

OBSTACLES TO GOOD PLANNING

Social pressures to own more "things."

The attitude that "more is better" regardless of the cost.

The use of credit to delay necessary decisions.

No surplus available to cope with rising prices and unexpected expenses.

We tend to offset increases in income by increasing our level of spending. That spending attitude is a real problem because it leads to:

THE DANGER POINT

When income barely equals outgo.

Break-even is not a living point but a decision point. If all the income is consumed in monthly expenses and something unusual happens, such as the family automobile breaking down, the result is additional indebtedness.

A decision is necessary at this point: *MAKE MORE MONEY OR SPEND LESS.*

Ideally this decision would be made before external pressures left few alternatives. Unfortunately when the pressure comes on, the credit card comes out. The result is a debt that cannot be paid. That limits the alternatives to treating the "symptoms." Some typical treatments are bill consolidation loans, additional credit, second mortgages, or a job for the wife. Those may provide temporary relief. But, unfortunately, since only the symptom has been treated, the problem still exists. It's only a matter of time until the symptoms reappear.

It is obviously better to cut expenses than to attempt to increase income. Unfortunately, it is also painful. The key? *Commitment.*

WHERE DO WE START?

Starting a budget is just like starting on a trip. You cannot set a course without first determining where you are.

Step one—The budget: what is the present level of spending?

Step two—Budget goals: Establish the "ideal" budget. In actuality, few people ever reach the ideal, but it is possible to establish the "now" condition by reviewing the ideal.

In establishing a budget, this trip will consist of comparing the present spending level with a guideline for balanced spending. The comparison will point out where adjustments should be made.

Once the budget is established, a control system must be incorporated that will keep spending on the "road." The system must be able to sound the alarm *before* overspending occurs.

THERE ARE ROAD HAZARDS

DISCOURAGEMENT

To complete the trip, one must keep going. A major problem is to develop a budget and then *not* follow it.

LEGALISM

Another problem is becoming legalistic and inflexible. Then the budget becomes a family weapon instead of a family tool. Becoming legalistic, incidentally, seems to occur at the same time the money runs out. If a road is blocked we usually have to take another route to get where we are going. Remain flexible to necessary changes.

OVERCORRECTION

When the money gets tight, the tendency is to eliminate clothes, entertainment, food, and other "expendables." That creates a pressure that is often relieved by overspending in other areas.

EVERYBODY NEEDS A BUDGET!

Financial bondage can result from a lack of money and overspending. But it can also be caused from the misuse of an abundance of money. Some families have enough money to be undisciplined and get away with it (financially speaking). But true financial freedom requires that we be good stewards. That is only possible with self-discipline.

A good plan requires *action* and *discipline* to make it work.

It may require sacrifice.

Begin *now*!

SECTION 2

WHERE ARE WE?

DETERMINING MONTHLY INCOME AND EXPENSES

THE PRESENT CONDITION

On the monthly Income and Expenses form (Figure 2.1 on page 13), compare actual monthly expenses with monthly income to determine present spending. (Note: You may need to keep a diary of expenses for a few months before you can accurately determine actual monthly expenses.)

To determine living cost, consider what represents a reasonable standard of living at your present income level. Reasonable, not total, sacrifices are necessary.

Therefore, when you set up your budget, include a reasonable amount for personal spending, e.g., clothes, savings, entertainment, recreation.

DETERMINE INCOME PER MONTH

NOTE: Use Form 1 (Monthly Income and Expenses sheet) for this section.

List all gross income (income before deductions) in the "Income Per Month" section on the Monthly Income and Expenses Sheet. Don't forget to include **commissions, bonuses, tips, and interest earned** that will be received over the next 12 months.

When income consists totally or partially of commissions or other fluctuating sources, average it for a year and divide by 12. Use a low yearly average, not a high average.

If you are paid weekly or bi-weekly, take the total yearly income and divide by 12.

Business expense reimbursements should not be considered family income. Avoid the trap of using expense money to buffer family spending or the result will be an indebtedness that cannot be paid.

WHAT IS "NET SPENDABLE INCOME"?

Net spendable income is that portion available for family spending. Some of your income does not belong to the family and therefore cannot be spent. For instance:

CATEGORY 1—Taxes: Federal withholding, Social Security, and state and local taxes must also be deducted from gross income. Self-employed individuals must not forget to set aside money for quarterly prepayments on taxes. Beware of the tendency to treat unpaid tax money as windfall profit.

CATEGORY 2—Charitable gifts: The term *tithe* means you give 10 percent of your total income to the church and other appropriate non-profit organizations. See *Your Finances in Changing Times*, Chapter 10, "Sharing—God's Way."

Other Deductions: Payroll deductions for insurance, credit union savings or debt payments, bonds, stock programs, retirement, and union dues can be handled in either of two ways.

1. Treat them as a deduction from gross income the same as the income taxes.

10

2. Include them in spendable income and deduct them from the proper category. This is preferred because it provides a more accurate picture of where the money is being spent.

EXAMPLE: A deduction is being made for credit union savings. This amount should be considered as a part of income with an expense shown under "Savings" for the same amount. This method makes it easier to see the overall effect the deduction has on the family budget.

NET SPENDABLE INCOME = GROSS INCOME MINUS TAXES AND MINUS CHARITABLE GIFTS.

HOW IS NET SPENDABLE INCOME BEING SPENT?

CATEGORY 3—Housing Expenses: All monthly expenses necessary to operate the home, including taxes, insurance, maintenance, and utilities. The amount used for utility payments should be an average monthly amount for the past 12 months.

If you cannot establish an accurate maintenance expense, use 5 percent of the monthly mortgage payment.

CATEGORY 4—Food Expenses: All grocery expenses, including paper goods and non-food products normally purchased at grocery stores. Include milk, bread, and items purchased in addition to regular shopping trips. Do not include eating out and daily lunches eaten away from home. If you do not know your actual food expenses, keep a detailed spending record for 30 to 45 days.

CATEGORY 5—Automobile Expenses: Includes payments, gas, oil, maintenance, and depreciation.

Depreciation is actually the money set aside to repair or replace the automobile. The minimum amount set aside should be sufficient to keep the car in decent repair and to replace it at least every four to five years.

If replacement funds are not available in the budget, the minimum allocation should be maintenance costs. Annual or semi-annual auto insurance payments should be set aside on a monthly basis, thereby avoiding the crisis of a neglected expense.

CATEGORY 6—Insurance: Includes all insurance, such as health, life, and disability not associated with the home or auto.

CATEGORY 7—Debts: Includes all monthly payments required to meet debt obligations. Home mortgage and automobile payments are not included here.

CATEGORY 8—Entertainment and Recreation: Vacation savings, camping trips, club dues, sporting equipment, hobby expenses, and athletic events. Don't forget Little League expense, booster clubs, and so on.

CATEGORY 9—Clothing: The average annual amount spent on clothes divided by 12. The minimum amount should be at least $10 per month per family member.

CATEGORY 10—Savings: Every family should allocate something for savings. A savings account can provide funds for emergencies and is a key element in good planning and financial freedom.

CATEGORY 11—Medical Expenses: Insurance deductibles, doctors' bills, eye glasses, drugs, orthodontist visits, and so on. Use a yearly average divided by 12 to determine a monthly amount.

CATEGORY 12—Miscellaneous: Specific expenses that do not seem to fit anywhere else, such as pocket allowance (coffee money), miscellaneous gifts, Christmas presents, toiletries, hair-cuts.

Miscellaneous spending is usually underestimated. A 30- to 45-day spending record is usually necessary to establish accurate present spending habits. Self-discipline is the key to controlling miscellaneous spending.

CATEGORY 13—School/Child Care: An ever–increasing segment of our population has expenses for private school and/or child care. This category must reflect those expenses. All other categories must be reduced to provide these funds.

CATEGORY 14—Investments: Individuals and families with surplus income in their budgets will have the opportunity to invest for retirement or other long-term goals. As debt-free status is achieved, more money can be diverted to this category.

UNALLOCATED SURPLUS INCOME

CATEGORY 15—Unallocated Surplus Income: Income from unbudgeted sources (garage sales, gifts, bonuses) can be kept in one's checking account and placed in this category. This section can be useful to keep track of surplus income, as well as to keep records for tax purposes. See page 41.

INCOME VS. EXPENSES

STEP ONE—Compile the expenses under each of the major categories (items 3 through 12) and note this as the total expense. Then in the space provided, subtract expenses from net spendable income.

STEP TWO—*If income is greater than expenses*, you need only to control spending to maximize the surplus. Section 5, The Guideline Budget, will help you to do this.

STEP THREE—*If expenses are greater than income*, a detailed analysis will be necessary to correct the situation and restore a proper balance. Proceed to the next section.

Figure 2.1 is an example of a family's current Monthly Income & Expenses. As you can see, they are currently overspending $90 per month. In addition, they do not have a balanced plan.

As you continue through the following sections you will be taught how to bring this hypothetical situation into balance and not show a negative monthly cash flow.

See Figure 6.1 (page 31) for comparision of the Existing Budget and a Monthly Guideline Budget.

MONTHLY INCOME & EXPENSES

GROSS INCOME PER MONTH		**$2,083**
Salary	2,083	
Interest		
Dividends		
Other		

LESS:

1. Tax (Est.-Incl. Fed., State,FICA)	500
2. Charitable Gifts	125
NET SPENDABLE INCOME	**1,458**

3. Housing		589
Mortgage (rent)	423	
Insurance		
Taxes		
Electricity	70	
Gas	20	
Water	16	
Sanitation		
Telephone	40	
Maintenance	20	
Other		

4. Food	230

5. Automobile(s)		285
Payments	140	
Gas & Oil	40	
Insurances	60	
License/Taxes	5	
Maint./Repair /Replace	40	

6. Insurance		39
Life	14	
Medical	25	
Other		

7.Debts		90
Credit Card	90	
Loans & Notes		
Other		

8. Entertainment & Recreation		100
Eating Out	35	
Baby Sitters		
Activities/Trips	20	
Vacation	10	
Other	35	

9. Clothing	50
10. Savings	0

11. Medical Exp.		20
Doctor	20	
Dentist		
Drugs		
Other		

12. Miscellaneous		145
Toiletry, cos.	19	
Beauty, barber	15	
Laundry, cl.	15	
Allow., lunches	16	
Subscriptions	20	
Gifts (incl. Christmas)	25	
Cash	35	
Other		

13. School/Child care	0
Tuition	
Materials	
Transportation	
Day Care	

14. Investments	0
TOTAL EXPENSES	**1,548**

INCOME VS. EXPENSES

Net Spendable Income	1,458
Less Explenses	1,548
	- 90

15. Unallocated Surplus Income[1]

[1]This category is used when surplus income is received. This would be kept in the checking account to be used within a few weeks; otherwise, it should be transferred to an allocated category. See page 41 for further information.

Figure 2.1

SECTION 3

SHORT-RANGE PLANNING

HANDLING THE VARIABLES BY SHORT-RANGE PLANNING

WHAT IS SHORT-RANGE PLANNING?

Budgeting for irregular expenses on a monthly basis. That includes fluctuating utility bills, auto maintenance, medical expenses, and clothing. See Figure 3.1.

EXAMPLE:1. By averaging utility bills over one year, money can be stored from low–use months to offset the cost of high–use months.

2. Annual or semi-annual insurance payments are met by establishing a monthly reserve.

Expenditures for clothing and medical and dental bills are other examples for which provision should be made. Those items normally are not purchased on a regular basis. Without the needed reserves, the result is often additional debt when those purchases must be made.

A vacation can be planned the same way. Plan what is needed for the coming year's vacation and divide the amount by 12 to determine what must be saved on a monthly basis.

Items such as automobiles, appliances, and household goods (furniture, rugs, drapes.) wear out or deteriorate over time. Periodic allocations should be made to replace those items as necessary.

Ideally, automobile depreciation and maintenance should be allocated on a monthly basis. That savings would then pay for maintenance, insurance, and replacement of the automobile (assuming the car is kept for 5 years or 100,000 miles).

A DANGER— The tendency in tight budgeting situations is to avoid maintenance and depreciation savings with the excuse that "we just can't afford it." Even if the full amount cannot be set aside, try to save something for those purposes. Depreciation is the same as any other expense. Without money to repair a car, the usual alternative is to replace it—on the time payment plan!

Failure to plan for short-range variables and depreciating items results in crisis planning. Control your expenditures; don't let them control you.

HOW TO DO THIS

Use the table illustrated in Figure 3.2 (page 18) to determine how much must be allocated to the various categories. For example, if automobile insurance is $480 per year, set aside $40 per month so that the bill can be paid when due.

Include those amounts in the proper categories when planning the total budget (use Form 2).

At the end of each month the allocated money not actually used is transferred to a savings account (illustrated in Figure 3.1). The savings ledger shows the various categories for which money is being saved (Form 6).

ESTABLISH ACCOUNT LIMITS. Each account should have a predetermined limit. Once that limit has been reached, no additional savings are necessary.

EXAMPLE: Assume $600 is the yearly total for medical expenses. Once the savings for medical reaches $600, the needed reserve has been met. Unless greater medical expenses are expected, savings beyond $600 are not necessary. Monthly funds then can be applied elsewhere until a medical expense occurs that reduces the amount in savings.

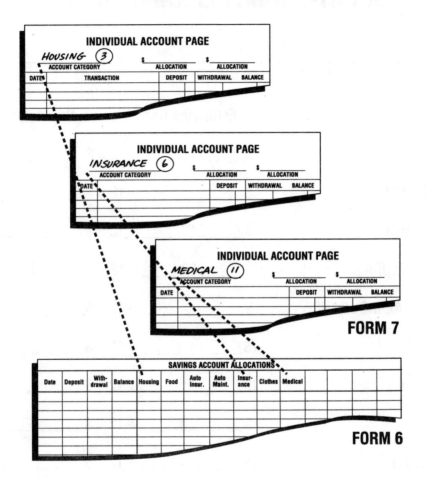

Figure 3.1

Remember, the plan is to establish a reserve for variables, depreciating items, maintenance, or special needs, such as fluctuating income. The savings account ledger divides the surplus by budget category.

BE FLEXIBLE. In starting a budget, it may be necessary to borrow from one account to supplement another. For example, if the car breaks down before a surplus is accumulated in the auto account, it may be necessary to borrow from the clothing or medical surpluses to pay for the car repair. However, to continue to do that month after month will defeat the long-range purpose in budgeting.

That purpose is to *plan ahead!*

SHORT-RANGE PLANNING SHEET

	Estimated Cost	Per Month
1. VACATION	$_____ ÷ 12 =	$_____
2. DENTIST	$_____ ÷ 12 =	$_____
3. DOCTOR	$_____240_____ ÷ 12 =	$_____20_____
4. AUTOMOBILE	$_____480_____ ÷ 12 =	$_____40_____
5. ANNUAL INSURANCE	$_____ ÷ 12 =	$_____
(Life)	($_____ ÷ 12 =	$_____)
(Health)	($_____ ÷ 12 =	$_____)
(Auto)	($_____720_____ ÷ 12 =	$_____60_____)
(Home)	($_____ ÷ 12 =	$_____)
6. CLOTHING	$_____600_____ ÷ 12 =	$_____50_____
7. INVESTMENTS	$_____ ÷ 12 =	$_____
8. OTHER	$_____ ÷ 12 =	$_____

Figure 3.2

SECTION 4

BUDGET PROBLEMS

BUDGET PROBLEM AREAS

BEWARE: Unforeseen problems can wreck your budget. Those include:

Bookkeeping Errors . . . Impulse Buying . . . Hidden Debts . . . Gifts

BOOKKEEPING ERRORS

An accurately balanced checkbook is a must. Even small errors result in big problems if they are allowed to compound. (A correct procedure is shown in Figure 4.1)

An inaccurate balance can result in an overdrawn account, as well as in significant bank charges.

Automatic banking systems create additional pitfalls. Automatic payment deductions must be subtracted from the checkbook ledger at the time they are paid by the bank.

EXAMPLE: An insurance premium is paid by automatic withdrawal on the 15th of each month. Since no statement or notice is received from the insurance company, you must be certain that on the 15th of every month the proper amount is deducted from your home checking account records.

The same would be true for automatic credit card payments or any other automatic withdrawal.

Direct deposits into checking accounts must also be noted in the home ledger at the proper time. *Don't forget* to include bank service charges in the home ledger (Form 7A).

Automatic Tellers: If you withdraw cash from your account using an outside/automatic teller, be sure you write it in your ledger and file the transaction record.

OTHER FACTORS IN KEEPING GOOD RECORDS

1. *Use a ledger–type checkbook rather than a stub type.* The ledger gives greater visibility and lends itself to fewer errors. I usually recommend using a checkbook that has a duplicate copy of the checks written. This eliminates not posting a check.

2. *Be certain all checks are accounted for.* All checks should be entered in the ledger when written. This entry must include the check number, amount, date, and assignee.

Tearing checks out of your checkbook for future use defeats many of the safeguards built into this system. I recommend that all checks be written from the checkbook only.

3. *One bookkeeper only.* When more than one individual attempts to maintain the record system, confusion usually results. If the system is in good order, either the husband or the wife can keep the records. The choice should be based on who can do the job best.

4. *Maintain a home ledger.* If all records are kept in a checkbook ledger, you run the risk of losing it. A home ledger eliminates this possibility and makes record keeping more orderly. Form 7A is used as your checkbook ledger sheet. This will be explained in Section 7.

5. *Balance the account every month—to the penny.* Never allow the home ledger and bank statement to disagree in balance. The two most common errors are arithmetic errors (addition or

CHECKBOOK BALANCE PROCEDURE

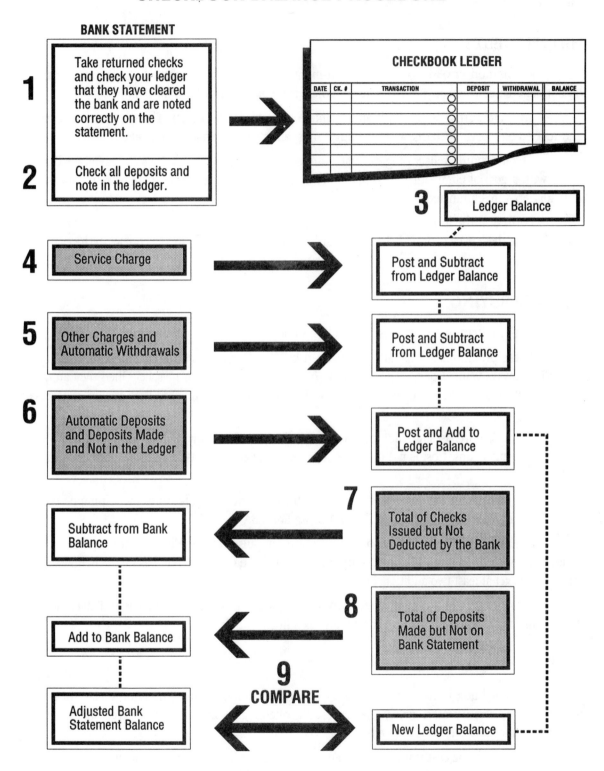

Figure 4.1

subtraction) and transposition errors (writing in the wrong amount). Use a calculator and balance the account *to the penny*.

HIDDEN DEBTS

A common error is to overlook non-monthly debts such as doctor bills, family loans, and bank notes. Thus, when payments come due, there is no budget allocation for them.

To avoid surprises, establish and maintain a list of debts in total. The list must be reviewed and revised on a periodic basis, and the budget must anticipate necessary payments.

The list should reflect progress made on debt payments and can serve as a "payoff goal" sheet. Begin with a goal of eliminating the smallest debt first. Then double up on the next debt, and so on, until all debts are eliminated.

Form 8 in the forms section is provided to list all outstanding debts. A copy is shown in Figure 4.2. Note that space is provided for the name and number of the person to contact in the event of a problem.

IMPULSE BUYING

Impulse items are unnecessary purchases made on the spur of the moment.

These purchases are usually rationalized by, "It was on sale, " "I was planning to buy it anyway," "I've always wanted one," "I just couldn't resist it," or, "I owe it to myself." Often they are made with a credit card because the cash isn't available. The net result is a little-used item and an unnecessary debt.

"Impulse purchases" are not restricted to small items. They range from homes, cars, and trips to unscheduled luncheons. Cost is not the issue; necessity is. Every purchase should be considered in light of the budget.

Discipline is the key to controlling impulse buying. If necessary, resort to the self-imposed discipline of the "impulse list" suggested in Figure 4.2 (see Form 8A).

Establish the discipline that, before buying on impulse, you will list the item on the impulse sheet, along with the date and the cost. Furthermore, wait 30 days before purchasing the item, and during that time get at least two additional prices.

If you feel you still need the item at the end of the 30 days and the money is available, then buy it. You will eliminate most impulse items by this discipline.

GIFTS

A major budget-buster in most families is overspending on gifts. Tradition dictates a gift for nearly every occasion. Unfortunately, the net result is often a gift someone else doesn't want, purchased with money that was needed for something else.

Many times the cost is increased because the gift is selected at the last moment. If gifts are a part of normal spending, budget for them and buy ahead—reasonably.

To bring the cost of gifts under control, consider doing the following.

1. Keep an event calendar for the year and budget ahead.

2. Determine not to buy any gifts on credit (especially Christmas gifts).

3. Initiate crafts within the family and make some of the needed gifts.

4. Draw family names for selected gifts rather than giving to everyone.

LIST OF DEBTS

TO WHOM OWED	CONTACT PHONE NO.	PAYOFF AMOUNT	PAYMENTS REMAINING	MONTHLY PAYMENT	DATE DUE

IMPULSE LIST

DATE	IMPULSE ITEM	1	2	3

Figure 4.2

THE GUIDELINE BUDGET

THE GUIDELINE BUDGET

WHAT IS A GUIDELINE BUDGET?

A guideline budget is family spending divided into percentages to help determine the proper balance in each category of the budget, e.g., housing, food, and automobile.

The primary use of the guideline is to indicate problem areas. It is not an absolute. The percentages are based on a family of four people with incomes ranging from $15,000 to $55,000 per year. Above or below those limits, the percentages may change according to family situations and needs. In the lower income levels, basic family needs will dominate the income distribution. Percentage guidelines are shown in Figure 5.1.

PURPOSE OF A GUIDELINE

The guideline is developed to determine a standard against which to compare present spending patterns. It will serve as a basis for determining areas of overspending that are creating the greatest problems. Additionally, it helps to determine where adjustments need to be made. If you are overspending, the percentage guideline can be used as a goal for budgeting. Although the percentages are guides only, and *not* absolute, they do help to establish upper levels of spending.

For instance: A family spending 40 percent or more of their net spendable income on housing will have difficulty balancing their budget. In most family incomes there is little flexibility to absorb excessive spending on housing (or automobiles).

GUIDELINE PERCENTAGES

The *net spendable income* is used to calculate the ideal spending for each budget category. Net spendable income is determined by subtracting your taxes and charitable contributions from your gross income. If taxes are known, then actual amounts can be used. For example, a family of four with an income of $25,000 per year would pay approximately 15.5 percent of gross income in taxes. (For a single person making $12,000 per year, the tax burden will be approximately 16.5 percent, based on the standard deduction.) In the example shown in Figure 5.2 on page 28, net spendable income is $1,553 per month. Thus for housing, 38 percent of N.S.I. equals $589 per month. Therefore, no more than $589 per month should be spent for housing, including payment, taxes, utilities, and upkeep.

Note that in some categories absolutes are impossible with variables such as utilities and taxes. You must adjust percentages within ranges under "Housing," "Food," and "Auto." Those three together cannot exceed 65 percent. Example: If 40 percent is used for housing, the percentage for food and auto must be reduced.

The next step? Budget Analysis.

PERCENTAGE GUIDE FOR FAMILY INCOME
(Family of Four)

Gross Income	15,000	25,000	35,000	45,000	55,000	65,000
1. Tithe	10%	10%	10%	10%	10%	10%
2. Taxes [1]	<8%>	13%	19%	20%	21%	25%
NET SPENDABLE [2]	14,700	19,250	24,850	31,500	37,950	42,250
3. Housing	38%	38%	34%	30%	27%	26%
4. Food	15%	12%	12%	12%	11%	10%
5. Auto	15%	15%	12%	12%	12%	11%
6. Insurance	5%	5%	5%	5%	5%	5%
7. Debts	5%	5%	5%	5%	5%	5%
8. Ent./Recreation	4%	5%	6%	6%	7%	7%
9. Clothing	4%	5%	5%	5%	6%	6%
10. Savings	5%	5%	5%	5%	5%	5%
11. Medical/Dental	5%	5%	4%	4%	4%	4%
12. Miscellaneous	4%	5%	5%	7%	7%	8%
13. School/Child Care [3]	10%	8%	6%	5%	5%	5%
14. Investments [4]	—	—	7%	9%	11%	13%
15. Unalloc. Surplus Inc. [5]	—	—	—	—	—	—

[1] Guideline percentages for tax category include taxes for Social Security, federal, and a small estimated amount for state, with only the standard deduction taken. At the 15,000 level of income the Earned Income Credit drastically reduces the tax burden and produces a sizeable refund.

[2] Begin figuring 100% from this figure, not from Gross Income. Categories 3-12 (and 14 in higher income brackets) should add up to 100% of Net Spendable Income.

[3] This category is added as a guide only. If you have this expense, the percentage shown must be deducted from other budget categories.

[4] This category is used for long-term investment planning such as college education or retirement.

[5] This category is used when surplus income is received. This would be kept in the checking account to be used within a few weeks; otherwise, it should be transferred to an allocated category.

Figure 5.1

BUDGET PERCENTAGE GUIDELINES

Salary for guideline= $25,000 / year

Gross Income Per Month	$2083				
1. Tax	(15.5% of Gross)	(2083)	=	$	322
2. Charitable gifts	(10% of Gross)	(2083)	=	$	208
Net Spendable Income		1553			
3. Housing	(38% of Net)	(1553)	=	$	589
4. Food	(12% of Net)	(1553)	=	$	186
5. Auto	(15% of Net)	(1553)	=	$	232
6. Insurance	(5% of Net)	(1553)	=	$	78
7. Debts	(5% of Net)	(1553)	=	$	78
8. Entertainment & Rec.	(5% of Net)	(1553)	=	$	78
9. Clothing	(5% of Net)	(1553)	=	$	78
10. Savings	(5% of Net)	(1553)	=	$	78
11. Medical	(5% of Net)	(1553)	=	$	78
12. Miscellaneous	(5% of Net)	(1553)	=	$	78
13. School / Child Care	(8% of Net)[1]	(_____)	=	$	_____
14. Investments	(0% of Net)[2]	(_____)	=	$	_____
Total (cannot exceed Net Spendable Income)				$	1553
15. Unallocated Surplus Income[3]		(N/A)	=	$	_____

[1]Note: This percentage has not been factored into the total percentages shown for net income.

[2]Note: Considering the given obligations at this income level, there is no surplus for investing long term.

[3]Note: This category is not part of the budget system but can be used to record and show disbursements of unallocated surplus income.

Figure 5.2

SECTION 6

BUDGET ANALYSIS

BUDGET ANALYSIS

After determining the present spending level (where you are), and reviewing the guideline percentages (where you should be), the task becomes one of developing a new budget that handles the areas of overspending. Keep in mind that the total expenditures must not exceed the net spendable income. If you have more spendable income than expenses, you need to control spending to maximize your surplus.

The Budget Analysis page (Figure 6.1) provides space for summarizing both actual expenses and guideline expenses on one sheet for working convenience. The total amounts of each category from the Monthly Income and Expenses sheet (Figure 2.1) and from the Budget Percentage Guidelines (Figure 5.1) should be transferred to the appropriate columns on the Budget Analysis page (Form 4).

STEP ONE: COMPARE

The *Existing Budget* and *Guideline* columns should be compared. Note the difference, plus or minus, in the *Difference* column. A negative notation indicates a deficit; a positive notation indicates a surplus. The budget shown is the actual spending of a typical family of four.

STEP TWO: ANALYZE

After comparing the *Existing* and *Guideline* columns, decisions must be made about overspending. It may be possible to reduce some areas to compensate for overspending in others. For example, if housing expenditures are more than 38 percent, it may be necessary to sacrifice in such areas as Entertainment and Recreation, Miscellaneous, and Automobiles. If debts exceed 5 percent, then the problems are compounded. Ultimately, the decision becomes one of where and how to cut back.

It is not necessary that your new budget fit the guideline budget. **It is necessary that your new budget not exceed Net Spendable Income.**

It is usually at this point that the husband-wife communication is so important. No one person can make a budget work, because it may involve a family financial sacrifice. Without a willingness to sacrifice and establish discipline, no budget will succeed.

Note the flexibility gained if the family is not in debt. That 5 percent is available for use somewhere else in the budget.

STEP THREE: DECIDE

Once the total picture is reviewed, it is necessary to decide where adjustments must be made and spending reduced. It may be necessary to consider a change in Housing, Automobiles, Insurance, or Child Care.

The minimum objective of any budget should be to meet the family's needs without creating any further debt.

If there are debt problems, then begin by destroying all credit cards and other sources of credit. It may be necessary to negotiate with creditors to pay smaller amounts per month. It's better to establish an amount you can pay than to promise an amount you cannot pay.

BUDGET ANALYSIS

Per Year $25,000   **Net Spendable Income Per Month $1510**

Per Month $2083

MONTHLY PAYMJENT CATEGORY	EXISTING BUDGET[1]	MONTHLY GUIDELINE BUDGET	DIFFERENCE + OR -	NEW MONTHLY BUDGET
1. Taxes	500	322	-178	322
2. Charitable Gifts	125	208	+83	208
NET SPENDABLE INCOME (Per Month)	$1458	$1553	$ +52	$1553
3. Housing	589	589	0	589
4. Food	230	186	-44	200
5. Auto	285	232	-53	260
6. Insurance	39	78	+39	39
7. Debts	90	78	-12	90
8. Entertainment / Recreation	100	78	-22	78
9. Clothing	50	78	+28	78
10. Savings	0	78	+78	78
11. Medical/ Dental	20	78	+58	63
12. Miscellaneous	145	78	-67	78
13. School/ Child Care[2]	0	120	+120	0
14. Investments	0	N/A	0	0
TOTALS (Items 3–12, 13, 14)	$1548	$1553		$1553
15. Unallocated Surplus Income[3]	0	N/A		+61

[1]The Existing Budget figures are taken from Figure 2.1 on page 13.

[2]This category not included in totals.

[3]This amount was derived from a garage sale. It is not part of your monthly budget. See page 41.

Figure 6.1

Beware of consolidation loans, refinancing, and more borrowing. They are not the solutions; they are merely "symptom" treatments. The solution comes from discipline, sacrifice, and trusting God to supply needs.

After a new budget has been determined, you are ready to proceed to the allocation and control system.

The adjustments were made as follows.

1. Taxes:	Taxes were reduced because actual taxes, with respect to gross income, were less than withholding when all deductions were considered. This was done by increasing the W-4 exemptions.
2. Charitable Gifts:	These were increased to 10 percent of gross income.
3. Housing:	No adjustment was made since the Housing allocation fit the family's present needs.
4. Food:	Note 16 percent of Net Spendable Income was being spent. A target amount of $200 was set. Perhaps this can be improved upon with wise shopping.
5. Auto:	Nearly 20 percent of Net Spendable Income was being spent. Transportation will be adjusted to $260 per month by reducing the insurance coverage.
6. Insurance:	No change. A close evaluation of insurance needs and types of insurance may be necessary in the future.
7. Debts:	More than 6 percent was allocated to existing debts. Credit cards were cancelled. This shows commitment and paves the way for paying off these debts totally in future months.
8. Entertainment & Recreation:	This category was reduced to $78 per month, at least until debts were paid. Caution: Don't cut this out; cut it back if necessary.
9. Clothing:	This category was underbudgeted. The allocation was increased to $78 per month.
10. Savings:	This was increased to $78. Get in the habit. It's the protection against future debt.
11. Medical:	This was another underallocation. It was increased to $63 per month.
12. Miscellaneous:	This category was reduced to $78 per month. If it's not enough, then you probably will have to reduce Entertainment and Recreation or Clothing.
13. School/Child Care:	No attempt was made to budget for this category. If funds are needed in your budget, the other categories must be adjusted accordingly.
14. Investments:	Once an adequate emergency fund is established, additional income may be invested for long-term goals.
15. Unallocated Surplus Income:	Since there is $61 surplus income this month from a garage sale, it will be placed in this category for future use as needed or directed to Debts reduction or Investments.

SECTION 7

THE CONTROL SYSTEM

ACCOUNTING - ALLOCATION - CONTROL

A budget that is not used is a waste of time and effort. The most common reason a budget is discarded is because it's too complicated.

The system described in this workbook is the simplest, yet most complete, possible.

KEEP IT SIMPLE

The Goal—Establish a level of spending for each category so that more money in does not mean more money to spend; and know where you are with respect to that level at all times.

This budget system is analogous to the old "envelope system." In the past, many employers paid earnings in cash. To control spending, families established an effective system by dividing the available money into the various budget categories (Housing, Food, Clothes), then holding it in individual envelopes.

As a need or payment came due, money was withdrawn from the appropriate envelope and spent.

The system was simple and, when used properly, quite effective for controlling spending. The rule was simple: When an envelope was empty, there was no more spending for that category. Money could be taken from another envelope, but a decision had to be made—immediately.

Since most families today get paid by check, and since holding cash in the home is not always advisable, a different cash allocation system is necessary.

It is important to know how much *should* be spent, how much is being spent, and how much is left to spend in each budget category. To accomplish this, account control pages have been substituted for envelopes. All the money is deposited into a checking account and account control pages are used to accomplish what the envelopes once accomplished. How much is put into each account (or envelope) from monies received during the month is determined from the Income Allocation sheet.

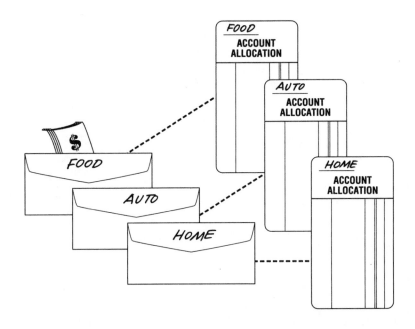

USE OF THE INCOME ALLOCATION PAGE (Form 5)

The purpose of the Income Allocation page is to divide Net Spendable Income among the various budget categories. It is simply a predetermined plan of how each paycheck or income source is going to be spent.

Once you have determined from the budget analysis how much can be spent in each category per month, write it in the *Monthly Allocation* column.

Next, divide the monthly allocation for each category (Housing, Food, Auto) by pay period.

EXAMPLE: Family income is received twice each month. Note that the mortgage payment is made on the 29th of the month, so the allocation must be divided in a manner to be sure that adequate funds are available at the time the payment is due. Utility and maintenance payments would have to be made from another pay period.

	ALLOCATION	PAY PERIOD	
HOUSING	$589	$423	$166
FOOD	$200	$100	$100
AUTO	$260	$160	$100
INSURANCE	$ 39	$ 14	$ 25

It is not mandatory that checks be divided evenly. The important thing is that when a payment is due the money is available. Therefore, some reserve funds from middle-of-the-month pay periods must be held to meet obligations that come due at the first of the month. Failure to do this is a common source of budget problems.

USE OF THE INDIVIDUAL ACCOUNT PAGES (Form 7) (Refer to Figure 7.1)

A separate account page is used for each budget category (Housing, Food, Auto) just as each had its own envelope under the cash system.

At the top of the page, the proper account title is entered (Housing, Food, Auto) together with the monthly allocation. Each account sheet has two blanks ($_____). These are used to write in your allocation for a twice–monthly pay period. If you are paid more frequently, just add more blanks ($_____). This will help you to remember how much to write in each pay period.

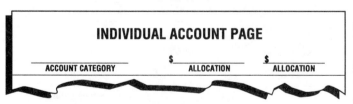

The purpose of the account sheet is to document ALL transactions for the month. The pay period allowance or allocation is shown as a deposit, and each time money is spent, it is shown as a withdrawal.

If funds are left at the end of the month, the account page is zeroed by transferring the money to the savings account. If an account runs short, then it may be necessary to transfer money from savings to the appropriate account. When an account is out of money, a decision must be made concerning how it is going to be treated.

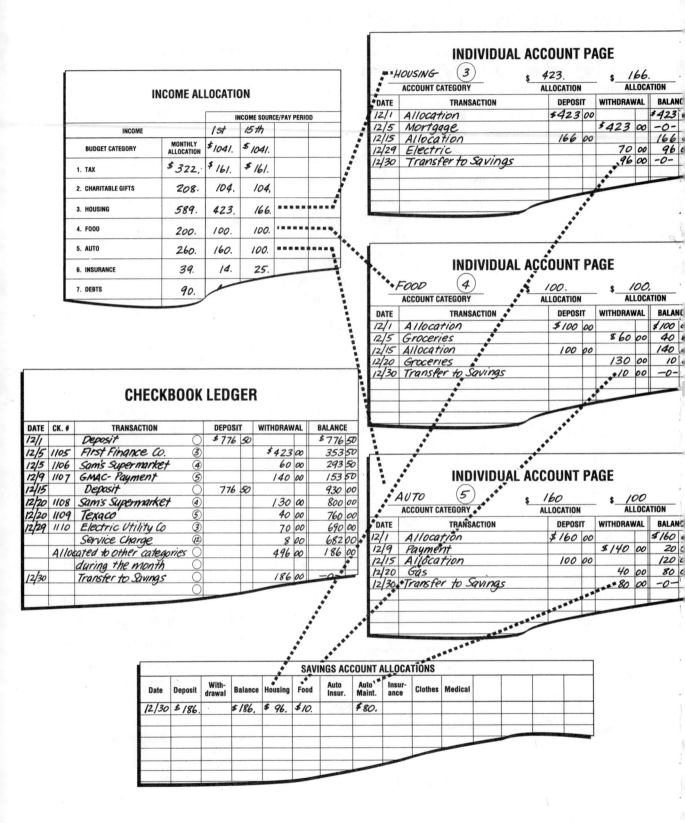

Figure 7.1

HOW TO USE THE BUDGET SYSTEM

A good budget system should be kept as simple as possible while still accomplishing its goal: *to tell you if you spend more than you allocated each month.* Remember that this system is analogous to using envelopes. If a specific amount of money is placed in the envelopes each month, you will know at a glance whether or not your budget balances. Obviously, with some non-monthly expenses to be budgeted the ledger system has to be a little more complicated, but don't *overcomplicate* it.

To help you better understand how to use the budget system, we will take one category (Housing) through a typical month's transactions.

INCOME ALLOCATION — FORM 5

BUDGET CATEGORY	MONTHLY ALLOCATION	INCOME SOURCE/PAY PERIOD	
		1st	15th
INCOME		$1041.	$1041.
1. TAX	$322.	$161.	$161.
2. CHARITABLE GIFTS	208.	104.	104.
3. HOUSING	589.	423.	166.
4. FOOD	200.	100.	100.
5. AUTO	260.	160.	100.
6. INSURANCE	39.	14.	25.
7. DEBTS	90.		

INDIVIDUAL ACCOUNT PAGE — FORM 7

AUTO ⑤   ACCOUNT CATEGORY $ 160 ALLOCATION $ 100 ALLOCATION

DATE	TRANSACTION	DEPOSIT	WITHDRAWAL	BALANCE
12/1	Allocation	$160 00		$160 00
12/9	Payment		$140 00	20 00
12/15	Allocation	100 00		120 00
12/20	Gas		40 00	80 00
12/30	Transfer to Savings		80 00	–0–

Figure 7.2

Figure 7.2 shows a typical family budget in which the gross income of $2083 per month is received in two pay periods of $1041 each.

PAY ALLOCATION— The two checks have been divided as evenly as possible among the necessary categories. For example, taxes are paid each pay period (remember, they are based on gross income). The Housing allocation of $589 is divided: $423 in the first pay period, $166 in the second.

HOUSING ALLOCATION—On the first pay period, a deposit of $423 is noted on the account page. On the fifth, the mortgage is paid and noted as a withdrawal, leaving a balance of $0.

Each transaction is noted similarly until, at the end of the month, a balance of $96 is left. This balance is then transferred to savings, as are month-end balances from the other account pages (Food, Savings). Hence, each account starts at zero the next month.

Many people prefer to leave the surplus funds from each category in their checking account rather than transfer them to a savings account. This is fine provided that you can discipline yourself not to spend the money just because it's easily accessible. Often the total cash reserves in checking are enough to qualify for free checking privileges, which more than offset any loss of interest in a savings account.

NOTE: In many cases, the housing account may have to carry a surplus forward to make the mortgage payment if it comes due on the first of the month.

USE OF THE CHECKBOOK LEDGER

To simplify your bookkeeping, I recommend using one of the Individual Account pages (Form 7) as a checkbook ledger. If you also use a checkbook that gives you a duplicate copy of each check written, it will reduce the number of steps in the bookkeeping process.

Note that the Checkbook Ledger (Form 7A) is just a slightly modified Form 7. Each deposit and withdrawal is recorded and the outstanding balance is shown. At the end of each month the ledger is balanced against the bank statement. Also, the total balance in the ledger is then compared to the balance on the budget account sheets.

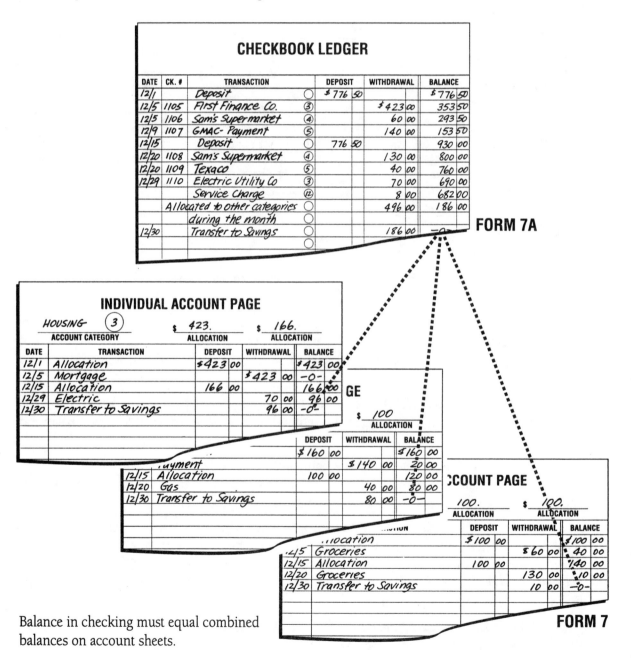

CHECKBOOK LEDGER

DATE	CK. #	TRANSACTION		DEPOSIT	WITHDRAWAL	BALANCE
12/1		Deposit	○	$776 50		$776 50
12/5	1105	First Finance Co.	③		$423 00	353 50
12/5	1106	Sam's Supermarket	④		60 00	293 50
12/9	1107	GMAC- Payment	⑤		140 00	153 50
12/15		Deposit	○	776 50		930 00
12/20	1108	Sam's Supermarket	④		130 00	800 00
12/20	1109	Texaco	⑤		40 00	760 00
12/29	1110	Electric Utility Co	③		70 00	690 00
		Service Charge	⑫		8 00	682 00
		Allocated to other categories	○		496 00	186 00
		during the month	○			
12/30		Transfer to Savings	○		186 00	-0-
			○			

FORM 7A

INDIVIDUAL ACCOUNT PAGE

HOUSING ③ $ 423. $ 166.
ACCOUNT CATEGORY   ALLOCATION   ALLOCATION

DATE	TRANSACTION	DEPOSIT	WITHDRAWAL	BALANCE
12/1	Allocation	$423 00		$423 00
12/5	Mortgage		$423 00	-0-
12/15	Allocation	166 00		166 00
12/29	Electric		70 00	96 00
12/30	Transfer to Savings		96 00	-0-

GE

$ 100
ALLOCATION

	DEPOSIT	WITHDRAWAL	BALANCE
	$160 00		$160 00
...ayment		$140 00	20 00
12/15 Allocation	100 00		120 00
12/20 Gas		40 00	80 00
12/30 Transfer to Savings		80 00	-0-

CCOUNT PAGE

100. $ 100.
ALLOCATION   ALLOCATION

...TION	DEPOSIT	WITHDRAWAL	BALANCE
...llocation	$100 00		$100 00
12/5 Groceries		$60 00	40 00
12/15 Allocation	100 00		140 00
12/20 Groceries		130 00	10 00
12/30 Transfer to Savings		10 00	-0-

FORM 7

Balance in checking must equal combined balances on account sheets.

If there are additional deposits or withdrawals from the bank statement recorded in the Checkbook Ledger, these must also be posted in the appropriate budget account sheets. For example, a service charge from the bank would be posted as an expense in the Checkbook Ledger and as a Miscellaneous expense in category 12 of the budget.

CHECKBOOK LEDGER

DATE	CK. #	TRANSACTION		DEPOSIT		WITHDRAWAL		BALANCE	
12/1		Deposit	○	$776	50			$776	50
12/5	1105	First Finance Co.	③			$423	00	353	50
12/5	1106	Sam's Supermarket	④			60	00	293	50
12/9	1107	GMAC- Payment	⑤			140	00	153	50
12/15		Deposit	○	776	50			930	00
12/20	1108	Sam's Supermarket	④			130	00	800	00
12/20	1109	Texaco	⑤			40	00	760	00
12/29	1110	Electric Utility Co	③			70	00	690	00
		Service Charge	⑫			8	00	682	00
		Allocated to other categories	○			496	00	186	00
		during the month	○						
12/30		Transfer to Savings	○			186	00	—0—	
			○						

FORM 7A

INDIVIDUAL ACCOUNT PAGE

Miscellaneous ⑫ $ 39. $ 39.
ACCOUNT CATEGORY   ALLOCATION   ALLOCATION

DATE	TRANSACTION	DEPOSIT		WITHDRAWAL		BALANCE	
12/1	Allocation	$ 39	00			$39	00
12/15	Allocation	39	00			78	00
12/30	Service charge			$ 8 00		70	00
12/30	Transfer to Savings			70	00	—0—	

FORM 7

Note that the circle (○) on Form 7A is used to indicate the category to which the check has been allocated in the budget. This is filled in only after the check has been recorded in the proper budget category.

CHECKING ACCOUNT NOTATION

The common practice with many budgeters is to write the checks, record (post) the checks in the home ledger (Figure 7.3), and then record the transactions in the budget account sheets at a later time. To insure that all checks are recorded in the account sheets, a notation of the category number should be made for each entry in the checkbook ledger in the appropriate block.

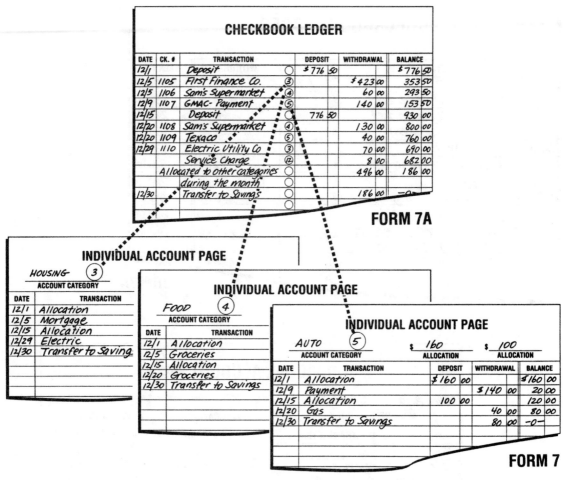

Figure 7.3

Keep in mind that the goal of the system is to establish a level of spending for each category and to know where you are with respect to that level.

The account pages ("envelopes") keep track of money in the checking account. The Savings Allocation page (Form 6) keeps track of money in the savings account. However, you may want to use a savings account page (or envelope) within the checking account to minimize transfers to and from the savings account.

Remember—the plan is to know what each dollar in the checking account is for and what each dollar in the savings account is for. When you spend money, you need to know which money is spent (clothes money, food money, gas money).

USE OF CATEGORY 15—SURPLUS INCOME

I have found in using the budget system myself that sometimes I had extra money available above that which I had budgeted. I could have transferred it to my Savings category, and often did if the money was to be used several months later. But if the money was going to be used within a few weeks, I wanted to leave it in the checking account. Since I didn't want it allocated to any of the regular monthly categories, I created a 15th category just to hold these surplus funds. This allowed me to keep each of the other categories constant each month. You may find this system helpful if you periodically have extra income that is unallocated. It also serves as a good record of income for tax purposes.

DISCIPLINE

In order to provide the necessary control, you must discipline yourself to spend money based on the bottom line of the applicable envelope and not based on the bottom line of the Checkbook Ledger.

POTENTIAL PROBLEM AREAS

CASH WITHDRAWALS—Many times miscellaneous expenditures for car expenses or gas are made with personal cash. In establishing a budget, it is important to develop some rules for self-discipline.

1. Separate personal cash into categories identical to the account pages. Use envelopes if necessary, but avoid spending gas money for lunches and grocery money for entertainment.

2. When all the money has been spent from a category (entertainment, lunches) *stop spending.*

3. Don't write checks for amounts in excess of actual purchases to get cash. Write another check and note it as "cash, personal."

CATEGORY MIXING—Don't try to make the record-keeping more complicated than necessary. This system should require no more than 30 minutes per week to maintain. If you choose to develop a more detailed breakdown of expenses and savings, wait until the budget has been in use at least six months.

AUTOMATIC OVERDRAFTS

Many banks offer an automatic overdraft protection service. Thus if you write a check in excess of what you have in your account, the bank will still honor it. On the surface this looks like a helpful service. However, it has been my experience that the overdraft protection tends to create a complacent attitude about balancing the account and encourages overdrafting. Since these charges are accrued to a credit account, you will end up paying interest on your overdrafts. I recommend that these services be avoided until the budgeting routine is well established. Perhaps by then they will be unnecessary.

BUDGETING ON A VARIABLE INCOME

One of the most difficult problems in budgeting is how to allocate monthly spending when your income fluctuates, as it often does on commission sales. The normal tendency is to spend the money as it comes in. This works great during the high income months but usually causes havoc during the lower income months.

Two suggestions will help anyone living on a fluctuating income. First, always separate any business-related expenses such as car maintenance, meals, or living accommodations from your normal household expenses. I recommend a separate checking account for business expenses and separate credit cards, if needed.

Second, you need to estimate what your (low) average income for one year will be and generate your monthly budget based on the "average" income per month. As the funds come in they need to be deposited in a special savings account and a salary drawn from the account. The effect is to ration the income over the year in relatively equal amounts that can be budgeted.

Remember that if you are self-employed, you will need to budget for payroll taxes on a quarterly basis. Failure to do this will result in a rather unpleasant visit with representatives of the Internal Revenue Service.

If you are beginning your budget during one of the lower income months, you may have to delay funding some of the variable expenses such as clothing, vacations, or dental. These can be funded later when the income allows.

WHAT IF YOU ARE PAID EVERY TWO WEEKS?

If you happen to be one of those families paid every two weeks rather than twice monthly, you will have two extra paychecks a year. I recommend using these paychecks to fund some of the non-monthly expenses such as car repair, vacation, or clothing. The same would be true of tax refunds, bonuses, and gifts.

SECTION 8

BEGIN NOW

MONTHLY INCOME & EXPENSES

GROSS INCOME PER MONTH _____
    Salary _____
    Interest _____
    Dividends _____
    Other _____

LESS:
1. Tax (Est.-Incl. Fed.,
    State,FICA) _____

2. Charitable Gifts _____

NET SPENDABLE INCOME _____

3. Housing
    Mortgage (rent) _____
    Insurance _____
    Taxes _____
    Electricity _____ _____
    Gas _____
    Water _____
    Sanitation _____
    Telephone _____
    Maintenance _____
    Other _____

4. Food _____

5. Automobile(s) _____
    Payments _____
    Gas & Oil _____
    Insurances _____
    License/Taxes _____
    Maint./Repair
    /Replace _____

6. Insurance _____
    Life _____
    Medical _____
    Other _____

7.Debts _____
    Credit Card _____
    Loans & Notes _____
    Other _____

8. Entertainment & Recreation _____
    Eating Out _____
    Baby Sitters _____
    Activities/Trips _____
    Vacation _____
    Other _____

9. Clothing _____

10. Savings _____

11. Medical Exp. _____
    Doctor _____
    Dentist _____
    Drugs _____
    Other _____

12. Miscellaneous _____
    Toiletry, cos. _____
    Beauty, barber _____
    Laundry, cl. _____
    Allow., lunches _____
    Subscriptions _____
    Gifts (incl.
    Christmas) _____
    Cash _____
    Other _____

13. School/Child care _____
    Tuition _____
    Materials _____
    Transportation _____
    Day Care _____

14. Investments _____

TOTAL EXPENSES _____

INCOME VS. EXPENSES
    Net Spendable Income _____
    Less Explenses _____

_____

15. Unallocated Surplus Income[1] _____

[1]This category is used when surplus income is received. This would be kept in the checking account to be used within a few weeks; otherwise, it should be transferred to an allocated category. See page 41 for further information.

FORM 1

MONTHLY INCOME & EXPENSES

GROSS INCOME PER MONTH _____
- Salary _____
- Interest _____
- Dividends _____
- Other _____

LESS:

1. Tax (Est.-Incl. Fed., State,FICA) _____

2. Charitable Gifts _____

NET SPENDABLE INCOME _____

3. Housing
- Mortgage (rent) _____
- Insurance _____
- Taxes _____
- Electricity _____
- Gas _____
- Water _____
- Sanitation _____
- Telephone _____
- Maintenance _____
- Other _____   _____

4. Food _____

5. Automobile(s) _____
- Payments _____
- Gas & Oil _____
- Insurances _____
- License/Taxes _____
- Maint./Repair /Replace _____

6. Insurance _____
- Life _____
- Medical _____
- Other _____

7. Debts _____
- Credit Card _____
- Loans & Notes _____
- Other _____

8. Entertainment & Recreation _____
- Eating Out _____
- Baby Sitters _____
- Activities/Trips _____
- Vacation _____
- Other _____

9. Clothing _____

10. Savings _____

11. Medical Exp. _____
- Doctor _____
- Dentist _____
- Drugs _____
- Other _____

12. Miscellaneous _____
- Toiletry, cos. _____
- Beauty, barber _____
- Laundry, cl. _____
- Allow., lunches _____
- Subscriptions _____
- Gifts (incl. Christmas) _____
- Cash _____
- Other _____

13. School/Child care _____
- Tuition _____
- Materials _____
- Transportation _____
- Day Care _____

14. Investments _____

TOTAL EXPENSES _____

INCOME VS. EXPENSES
Net Spendable Income _____
Less Explenses _____

_____

15. Unallocated Surplus Income[1] _____

[1]This category is used when surplus income is received. This would be kept in the checking account to be used within a few weeks; otherwise, it should be transferred to an allocated category. See page 41 for further information.

FORM 1

MONTHLY INCOME & EXPENSES

GROSS INCOME PER MONTH _____
    Salary _____
    Interest _____
    Dividends _____
    Other _____

LESS:

1. Tax (Est.-Incl. Fed., State,FICA) _____

2. Charitable Gifts _____

NET SPENDABLE INCOME _____

3. Housing
    Mortgage (rent) _____
    Insurance _____
    Taxes _____
    Electricity _____ _____
    Gas _____
    Water _____
    Sanitation _____
    Telephone _____
    Maintenance _____
    Other _____

4. Food _____

5. Automobile(s) _____
    Payments _____
    Gas & Oil _____
    Insurances _____
    License/Taxes _____
    Maint./Repair /Replace _____

6. Insurance _____
    Life _____
    Medical _____
    Other _____

7.Debts _____
    Credit Card _____
    Loans & Notes _____
    Other _____

8. Entertainment & Recreation _____
    Eating Out _____
    Baby Sitters _____
    Activities/Trips _____
    Vacation _____
    Other _____

9. Clothing _____

10. Savings _____

11. Medical Exp. _____
    Doctor _____
    Dentist _____
    Drugs _____
    Other _____

12. Miscellaneous _____
    Toiletry, cos. _____
    Beauty, barber _____
    Laundry, cl. _____
    Allow., lunches _____
    Subscriptions _____
    Gifts (incl. Christmas) _____
    Cash _____
    Other _____

13. School/Child care _____
    Tuition _____
    Materials _____
    Transportation _____
    Day Care _____

14. Investments _____

TOTAL EXPENSES _____

INCOME VS. EXPENSES
    Net Spendable Income _____
    Less Explenses _____

_____

15. Unallocated Surplus Income[1] _____

[1]This category is used when surplus income is received. This would be kept in the checking account to be used within a few weeks; otherwise, it should be transferred to an allocated category. See page 41 for further information.

FORM 1

MONTHLY INCOME & EXPENSES

GROSS INCOME PER MONTH _____
    Salary _____
    Interest _____
    Dividends _____
    Other _____

LESS:
1. Tax (Est.-Incl. Fed.,
    State, FICA) _____

2. Charitable Gifts _____

NET SPENDABLE INCOME _____

3. Housing
    Mortgage (rent) _____
    Insurance _____
    Taxes _____
    Electricity _____
    Gas _____
    Water _____
    Sanitation _____
    Telephone _____
    Maintenance _____
    Other _____

4. Food _____

5. Automobile(s) _____
    Payments _____
    Gas & Oil _____
    Insurances _____
    License/Taxes _____
    Maint./Repair
    /Replace _____

6. Insurance _____
    Life _____
    Medical _____
    Other _____

7. Debts _____
    Credit Card _____
    Loans & Notes _____
    Other _____

8. Entertainment & Recreation _____
    Eating Out _____
    Baby Sitters _____
    Activities/Trips _____
    Vacation _____
    Other _____

9. Clothing _____

10. Savings _____

11. Medical Exp. _____
    Doctor _____
    Dentist _____
    Drugs _____
    Other _____

12. Miscellaneous _____
    Toiletry, cos. _____
    Beauty, barber _____
    Laundry, cl. _____
    Allow., lunches _____
    Subscriptions _____
    Gifts (incl.
    Christmas) _____
    Cash _____
    Other _____

13. School/Child care _____
    Tuition _____
    Materials _____
    Transportation _____
    Day Care _____

14. Investments _____

TOTAL EXPENSES _____

INCOME VS. EXPENSES
    Net Spendable Income _____
    Less Explenses _____

_____

15. Unallocated Surplus Income[1] _____

[1]This category is used when surplus income is received. This would be kept in the checking account to be used within a few weeks; otherwise, it should be transferred to an allocated category. See page 41 for further information.

FORM 1

VARIABLE EXPENSE PLANNING

Plan for those expenses that are not paid on a regular monthly basis by estimating the yearly cost and determining the monthly amount needed to be set aside for that expense. A helpful formula is to allow the previous year's expense and add 5 percent.

	Estimated Cost	Per Month
1. VACATION	$_____	÷ 12 = $_____
2. DENTIST	$_____	÷ 12 = $_____
3. DOCTOR	$_____	÷ 12 = $_____
4. AUTOMOBILE	$_____	÷ 12 = $_____
5. ANNUAL INSURANCE	$_____	÷ 12 = $_____
(Life)	($_____	÷ 12 = $_____)
(Health)	($_____	÷ 12 = $_____)
(Auto)	($_____	÷ 12 = $_____)
(Home)	($_____	÷ 12 = $_____)
6. CLOTHING	$_____	÷ 12 = $_____
7. INVESTMENTS	$_____	÷ 12 = $_____
8. OTHER	$_____	÷ 12 = $_____

VARIABLE EXPENSE PLANNING

Plan for those expenses that are not paid on a regular monthly basis by estimating the yearly cost and determining the monthly amount needed to be set aside for that expense. A helpful formula is to allow the previous year's expense and add 5 percent.

	Estimated Cost	Per Month
1. VACATION	$_____	÷ 12 = $_____
2. DENTIST	$_____	÷ 12 = $_____
3. DOCTOR	$_____	÷ 12 = $_____
4. AUTOMOBILE	$_____	÷ 12 = $_____
5. ANNUAL INSURANCE	$_____	÷ 12 = $_____
(Life)	($_____	÷ 12 = $_____)
(Health)	($_____	÷ 12 = $_____)
(Auto)	($_____	÷ 12 = $_____)
(Home)	($_____	÷ 12 = $_____)
6. CLOTHING	$_____	÷ 12 = $_____
7. INVESTMENTS	$_____	÷ 12 = $_____
8. OTHER	$_____	÷ 12 = $_____

FORM 2

VARIABLE EXPENSE PLANNING

Plan for those expenses that are not paid on a regular monthly basis by estimating the yearly cost and determining the monthly amount needed to be set aside for that expense. A helpful formula is to allow the previous year's expense and add 5 percent.

	Estimated Cost	Per Month
1. VACATION	$_____	÷ 12 = $_____
2. DENTIST	$_____	÷ 12 = $_____
3. DOCTOR	$_____	÷ 12 = $_____
4. AUTOMOBILE	$_____	÷ 12 = $_____
5. ANNUAL INSURANCE	$_____	÷ 12 = $_____
(Life)	($_____	÷ 12 = $_____)
(Health)	($_____	÷ 12 = $_____)
(Auto)	($_____	÷ 12 = $_____)
(Home)	($_____	÷ 12 = $_____)
6. CLOTHING	$_____	÷ 12 = $_____
7. INVESTMENTS	$_____	÷ 12 = $_____
8. OTHER	$_____	÷ 12 = $_____

VARIABLE EXPENSE PLANNING

Plan for those expenses that are not paid on a regular monthly basis by estimating the yearly cost and determining the monthly amount needed to be set aside for that expense. A helpful formula is to allow the previous year's expense and add 5 percent.

	Estimated Cost	Per Month
1. VACATION	$_____	÷ 12 = $_____
2. DENTIST	$_____	÷ 12 = $_____
3. DOCTOR	$_____	÷ 12 = $_____
4. AUTOMOBILE	$_____	÷ 12 = $_____
5. ANNUAL INSURANCE	$_____	÷ 12 = $_____
(Life)	($_____	÷ 12 = $_____)
(Health)	($_____	÷ 12 = $_____)
(Auto)	($_____	÷ 12 = $_____)
(Home)	($_____	÷ 12 = $_____)
6. CLOTHING	$_____	÷ 12 = $_____
7. INVESTMENTS	$_____	÷ 12 = $_____
8. OTHER	$_____	÷ 12 = $_____

VARIABLE EXPENSE PLANNING

Plan for those expenses that are not paid on a regular monthly basis by estimating the yearly cost and determining the monthly amount needed to be set aside for that expense. A helpful formula is to allow the previous year's expense and add 5 percent.

	Estimated Cost	Per Month
1. VACATION	$_____	÷ 12 = $_____
2. DENTIST	$_____	÷ 12 = $_____
3. DOCTOR	$_____	÷ 12 = $_____
4. AUTOMOBILE	$_____	÷ 12 = $_____
5. ANNUAL INSURANCE	$_____	÷ 12 = $_____
(Life)	($_____	÷ 12 = $_____)
(Health)	($_____	÷ 12 = $_____)
(Auto)	($_____	÷ 12 = $_____)
(Home)	($_____	÷ 12 = $_____)
6. CLOTHING	$_____	÷ 12 = $_____
7. INVESTMENTS	$_____	÷ 12 = $_____
8. OTHER	$_____	÷ 12 = $_____

FORM 2

VARIABLE EXPENSE PLANNING

Plan for those expenses that are not paid on a regular monthly basis by estimating the yearly cost and determining the monthly amount needed to be set aside for that expense. A helpful formula is to allow the previous year's expense and add 5 percent.

	Estimated Cost	**Per Month**
1. VACATION	$_____	÷ 12 = $_____
2. DENTIST	$_____	÷ 12 = $_____
3. DOCTOR	$_____	÷ 12 = $_____
4. AUTOMOBILE	$_____	÷ 12 = $_____
5. ANNUAL INSURANCE	$_____	÷ 12 = $_____
(Life)	($_____	÷ 12 = $_____)
(Health)	($_____	÷ 12 = $_____)
(Auto)	($_____	÷ 12 = $_____)
(Home)	($_____	÷ 12 = $_____)
6. CLOTHING	$_____	÷ 12 = $_____
7. INVESTMENTS	$_____	÷ 12 = $_____
8. OTHER	$_____	÷ 12 = $_____

BUDGET PERCENTAGE GUIDELINES

Salary for guideline = _____ **/year**[1]

Gross Income Per Month_____

    1. Taxes   (____% of Gross) (_____) = $_____

    2. Charitable gifts (____% of Gross) (_____) = $_____

Net Spendable Income

    3. Housing   (____% of Net)   (_____) = $_____

    4. Food   (____% of Net)   (_____) = $_____

    5. Automobile(s)   (____% of Net)   (_____) = $_____

    6. Insurance   (____% of Net)   (_____) = $_____

    7. Debts   (____% of Net)   (_____) = $_____

    8. Entertainment   (____% of Net)   (_____) = $_____
        & Recreation

    9. Clothing   (____% of Net)   (_____) = $_____

    10. Savings   (____% of Net)   (_____) = $_____

    11. Medical   (____% of Net)   (_____) = $_____

    12. Miscellaneous (____% of Net)   (_____) = $_____

    13. School/Child Care (____% of Net)   (_____) = $_____

    14. Investments   (____% of Net)   (_____) = $_____

Total   **(cannot exceed Net Spendable Income)**

    15. Unallocated Surplus Income   (____N/A____) = $_____

[1]Refer to page 27 for percentage guidelines.

FORM 3

BUDGET PERCENTAGE GUIDELINES

Salary for guideline = _____ /year[1]

Gross Income Per Month_____

    1. Taxes   (____% of Gross)   (_____) = $_____

    2. Charitable gifts   (____% of Gross)   (_____) = $_____

Net Spendable Income

    3. Housing   (____% of Net)   (_____) = $_____

    4. Food   (____% of Net)   (_____) = $_____

    5. Automobile(s)   (____% of Net)   (_____) = $_____

    6. Insurance   (____% of Net)   (_____) = $_____

    7. Debts   (____% of Net)   (_____) = $_____

    8. Entertainment   (____% of Net)   (_____) = $_____
           & Recreation

    9. Clothing   (____% of Net)   (_____) = $_____

    10. Savings   (____% of Net)   (_____) = $_____

    11. Medical   (____% of Net)   (_____) = $_____

    12. Miscellaneous   (____% of Net)   (_____) = $_____

    13. School/Child Care   (____% of Net)   (_____) = $_____

    14. Investments   (____% of Net)   (_____) = $_____

Total   (cannot exceed Net Spendable Income)

    15. Unallocated Surplus Income   (____N/A____) = $_____

[1]Refer to page 27 for percentage guidelines.

FORM 3

BUDGET PERCENTAGE GUIDELINES

Salary for guideline = _____/year[1]

Gross Income Per Month_____

    1. Taxes   (___% of Gross) (_____) = $_____

    2. Charitable gifts   (___% of Gross) (_____) = $_____

Net Spendable Income

    3. Housing   (___% of Net)   (_____) = $_____

    4. Food   (___% of Net)   (_____) = $_____

    5. Automobile(s)   (___% of Net)   (_____) = $_____

    6. Insurance   (___% of Net)   (_____) = $_____

    7. Debts   (___% of Net)   (_____) = $_____

    8. Entertainment   (___% of Net)   (_____) = $_____
       & Recreation

    9. Clothing   (___% of Net)   (_____) = $_____

    10. Savings   (___% of Net)   (_____) = $_____

    11. Medical   (___% of Net)   (_____) = $_____

    12. Miscellaneous   (___% of Net)   (_____) = $_____

    13. School/Child Care (___% of Net)   (_____) = $_____

    14. Investments   (___% of Net)   (_____) = $_____

Total   **(cannot exceed Net Spendable Income)**

    15. Unallocated Surplus Income   (___N/A___) = $_____

[1]Refer to page 27 for percentage guidelines.

FORM 3

BUDGET PERCENTAGE GUIDELINES

Salary for guideline = _____/year[1]

Gross Income Per Month_____

1. Taxes	(____% of Gross)	(_____)	= $_____
2. Charitable gifts	(____% of Gross)	(_____)	= $_____

Net Spendable Income

3. Housing	(____% of Net)	(_____)	= $_____
4. Food	(____% of Net)	(_____)	= $_____
5. Automobile(s)	(____% of Net)	(_____)	= $_____
6. Insurance	(____% of Net)	(_____)	= $_____
7. Debts	(____% of Net)	(_____)	= $_____
8. Entertainment & Recreation	(____% of Net)	(_____)	= $_____
9. Clothing	(____% of Net)	(_____)	= $_____
10. Savings	(____% of Net)	(_____)	= $_____
11. Medical	(____% of Net)	(_____)	= $_____
12. Miscellaneous	(____% of Net)	(_____)	= $_____
13. School/Child Care	(____% of Net)	(_____)	= $_____
14. Investments	(____% of Net)	(_____)	= $_____

Total   (cannot exceed Net Spendable Income)

15. Unallocated Surplus Income   (____N/A____) = $_____

[1]Refer to page 27 for percentage guidelines.

FORM 3

BUDGET ANALYSIS

Per Year _____ **Net Spendable Income Per Month** _____

Per Month _____

MONTHLY PAYMENT CATEGORY	EXISTING BUDGET	MONTHLY GUIDELINE BUDGET	DIFFERENCE + OR -	NEW MONTHLY BUDGET
1. Taxes				
2. Charitable Gifts				
NET SPENDABLE INCOME (Per Month)	$_____	$_____	$_____	$_____
3. Housing				
4. Food				
5. Automobile(s)				
6. Insurance				
7. Debts				
8. Entertainment / Recreation				
9. Clothing				
10. Savings				
11. Medical/Dental				
12. Miscellaneous				
13. School/Child Care				
14. Investments				
TOTALS (Items 3–14)	$_____	$_____		$_____

| 15. Unallocated Surplus Income | $_____ | $_____ | | $_____ |

FORM 4

BUDGET ANALYSIS

Per Year _____   **Net Spendable Income Per Month** _____

Per Month _____

MONTHLY PAYMENT CATEGORY	EXISTING BUDGET	MONTHLY GUIDELINE BUDGET	DIFFERENCE + OR -	NEW MONTHLY BUDGET
1. Taxes				
2. Charitable Gifts				
NET SPENDABLE INCOME (Per Month)	$_____	$_____	$_____	$_____
3. Housing				
4. Food				
5. Automobile(s)				
6. Insurance				
7. Debts				
8. Entertainment / Recreation				
9. Clothing				
10. Savings				
11. Medical/Dental				
12. Miscellaneous				
13. School/Child Care				
14. Investments				
TOTALS (Items 3–14)	$_____	$_____		$_____
15. Unallocated Surplus Income	$_____	$_____		$_____

BUDGET ANALYSIS

Per Year _____   **Net Spendable Income Per Month** _____

Per Month _____

MONTHLY PAYMENT CATEGORY	EXISTING BUDGET	MONTHLY GUIDELINE BUDGET	DIFFERENCE + OR -	NEW MONTHLY BUDGET
1. Taxes				
2. Charitable Gifts				
NET SPENDABLE INCOME (Per Month)	$_____	$_____	$_____	$_____
3. Housing				
4. Food				
5. Automobile(s)				
6. Insurance				
7. Debts				
8. Entertainment / Recreation				
9. Clothing				
10. Savings				
11. Medical/Dental				
12. Miscellaneous				
13. School/Child Care				
14. Investments				
TOTALS (Items 3–14)	$_____	$_____		$_____
15. Unallocated Surplus Income	$_____	$_____		$_____

BUDGET ANALYSIS

Per Year _____   **Net Spendable Income Per Month** _____

Per Month _____

MONTHLY PAYMENT CATEGORY	EXISTING BUDGET	MONTHLY GUIDELINE BUDGET	DIFFERENCE + OR -	NEW MONTHLY BUDGET
1. Taxes				
2. Charitable Gifts				
NET SPENDABLE INCOME (Per Month)	$_____	$_____	$_____	$_____
3. Housing				
4. Food				
5. Automobile(s)				
6. Insurance				
7. Debts				
8. Entertainment / Recreation				
9. Clothing				
10. Savings				
11. Medical/Dental				
12. Miscellaneous				
13. School/Child Care				
14. Investments				
TOTALS (Items 3–14)	$_____	$_____		$_____
15. Unallocated Surplus Income	$_____	$_____		$_____

INCOME ALLOCATION

		INCOME SOURCE/PAY PERIOD			
INCOME					
BUDGET CATEGORY	**MONTHLY ALLOCATION**				
1. Taxes					
2. Charitable Gifts					
3. Housing					
4. Food					
5. Automobile(s)					
6. Insurance					
7. Debts					
8. Entertainment / Recreation					
9. Clothing					
10. Savings					
11. Medical / Dental					
12. Miscellaneous					
13. School / Child Care					
14. Investments					
15. Unallocated Surplus Income					

FORM 5

INCOME ALLOCATION

		INCOME SOURCE/PAY PERIOD			
INCOME					
BUDGET CATEGORY	**MONTHLY ALLOCATION**				
1. Taxes					
2. Charitable Gifts					
3. Housing					
4. Food					
5. Automobile(s)					
6. Insurance					
7. Debts					
8. Entertainment/Recreation					
9. Clothing					
10. Savings					
11. Medical/Dental					
12. Miscellaneous					
13. School/Child Care					
14. Investments					
15. Unallocated Surplus Income					

INCOME ALLOCATION

INCOME		INCOME SOURCE/PAY PERIOD			
BUDGET CATEGORY	**MONTHLY ALLOCATION**				
1. Taxes					
2. Charitable Gifts					
3. Housing					
4. Food					
5. Automobile(s)					
6. Insurance					
7. Debts					
8. Entertainment/Recreation					
9. Clothing					
10. Savings					
11. Medical/Dental					
12. Miscellaneous					
13. School/Child Care					
14. Investments					
15. Unallocated Surplus Income					

FORM 5

INCOME ALLOCATION

INCOME		INCOME SOURCE/PAY PERIOD			
BUDGET CATEGORY	**MONTHLY ALLOCATION**				
1. Taxes					
2. Charitable Gifts					
3. Housing					
4. Food					
5. Automobile(s)					
6. Insurance					
7. Debts					
8. Entertainment/Recreation					
9. Clothing					
10. Savings					
11. Medical/Dental					
12. Miscellaneous					
13. School/Child Care					
14. Investments					
15. Unallocated Surplus Income					

FORM 5

SAVINGS ACCOUNT ALLOCATIONS

Date	Deposit	With-drawal	Balance	Housing	Food	Auto Insur.	Auto Maint.	Insur-ance	Clothes	Medical			

FORM 6

SAVINGS ACCOUNT ALLOCATIONS

Date	Deposit	With-drawal	Balance	Housing	Food	Auto Insur.	Auto Maint.	Insur-ance	Clothes	Medical				

FORM 6

SAVINGS ACCOUNT ALLOCATIONS

Date	Deposit	With-drawal	Balance	Housing	Food	Auto Insur.	Auto Maint.	Insur-ance	Clothes	Medical															

FORM 6

SAVINGS ACCOUNT ALLOCATIONS

Date	Deposit	With-drawal	Balance	Housing	Food	Auto Insur.	Auto Maint.	Insur-ance	Clothes	Medical			

FORM 6

SAVINGS ACCOUNT ALLOCATIONS

Date	Deposit	With-drawal	Balance	Housing	Food	Auto Insur.	Auto Maint.	Insur-ance	Clothes	Medical			

FORM 6

SAVINGS ACCOUNT ALLOCATIONS

Date	Deposit	With-drawal	Balance	Housing	Food	Auto Insur.	Auto Maint.	Insur-ance	Clothes	Medical			

FORM 6

INDIVIDUAL ACCOUNT PAGE

		$		$	
	ACCOUNT CATEGORY	ALLOCATION		ALLOCATION	

DATE	TRANSACTION	DEPOSIT		WITHDRAWAL		BALANCE	

INDIVIDUAL ACCOUNT PAGE

	ACCOUNT CATEGORY		$ ALLOCATION			$ ALLOCATION	
DATE	TRANSACTION	DEPOSIT		WITHDRAWAL		BALANCE	

INDIVIDUAL ACCOUNT PAGE

$ _____

$ _____

ACCOUNT CATEGORY		ALLOCATION		ALLOCATION	

DATE	TRANSACTION	DEPOSIT		WITHDRAWAL		BALANCE	

FORM 7

INDIVIDUAL ACCOUNT PAGE

	ACCOUNT CATEGORY	$ _____ ALLOCATION		$ _____ ALLOCATION

DATE	TRANSACTION	DEPOSIT		WITHDRAWAL		BALANCE	

FORM 7

INDIVIDUAL ACCOUNT PAGE

	ACCOUNT CATEGORY	$ ALLOCATION	$ ALLOCATION

DATE	TRANSACTION	DEPOSIT	WITHDRAWAL		BALANCE	

FORM 7

INDIVIDUAL ACCOUNT PAGE

		$		$	
	ACCOUNT CATEGORY	ALLOCATION		ALLOCATION	

DATE	TRANSACTION	DEPOSIT		WITHDRAWAL		BALANCE	

FORM 7

INDIVIDUAL ACCOUNT PAGE

		$ _____		$ _____	
ACCOUNT CATEGORY		**ALLOCATION**		**ALLOCATION**	

DATE	TRANSACTION	DEPOSIT	WITHDRAWAL	BALANCE	

FORM 7

INDIVIDUAL ACCOUNT PAGE

ACCOUNT CATEGORY	$ ALLOCATION	$ ALLOCATION

DATE	TRANSACTION	DEPOSIT	WITHDRAWAL	BALANCE	

FORM 7

INDIVIDUAL ACCOUNT PAGE

		$		$	
	ACCOUNT CATEGORY	ALLOCATION		ALLOCATION	

DATE	TRANSACTION	DEPOSIT		WITHDRAWAL		BALANCE	

INDIVIDUAL ACCOUNT PAGE

ACCOUNT CATEGORY		$ ALLOCATION		$ ALLOCATION

DATE	TRANSACTION	DEPOSIT	WITHDRAWAL	BALANCE

FORM 7

INDIVIDUAL ACCOUNT PAGE

ACCOUNT CATEGORY		$ ALLOCATION		$ ALLOCATION

DATE	TRANSACTION	DEPOSIT		WITHDRAWAL		BALANCE	

INDIVIDUAL ACCOUNT PAGE

	ACCOUNT CATEGORY		\$ ALLOCATION			\$ ALLOCATION	
DATE	TRANSACTION		DEPOSIT	WITHDRAWAL		BALANCE	

INDIVIDUAL ACCOUNT PAGE

ACCOUNT CATEGORY	$ ALLOCATION	$ ALLOCATION

DATE	TRANSACTION	DEPOSIT		WITHDRAWAL		BALANCE	

FORM 7

INDIVIDUAL ACCOUNT PAGE

$ _____	$ _____
ACCOUNT CATEGORY	ALLOCATION	ALLOCATION

DATE	TRANSACTION	DEPOSIT	WITHDRAWAL	BALANCE

FORM 7

INDIVIDUAL ACCOUNT PAGE

ACCOUNT CATEGORY		$ _____ ALLOCATION		$ _____ ALLOCATION	

DATE	TRANSACTION	DEPOSIT		WITHDRAWAL		BALANCE	

FORM 7

INDIVIDUAL ACCOUNT PAGE

ACCOUNT CATEGORY		$ _____ ALLOCATION		$ _____ ALLOCATION	

DATE	TRANSACTION	DEPOSIT		WITHDRAWAL		BALANCE	

INDIVIDUAL ACCOUNT PAGE

| | | | $_____ | | | | $_____ | |
| | ACCOUNT CATEGORY | | ALLOCATION | | | | ALLOCATION | |

DATE	TRANSACTION	DEPOSIT		WITHDRAWAL		BALANCE	

INDIVIDUAL ACCOUNT PAGE

	ACCOUNT CATEGORY	$ ALLOCATION		$ ALLOCATION	

DATE	TRANSACTION	DEPOSIT	WITHDRAWAL	BALANCE	

FORM 7

INDIVIDUAL ACCOUNT PAGE

$ _____ $ _____

| ACCOUNT CATEGORY | ALLOCATION | ALLOCATION |

DATE	TRANSACTION	DEPOSIT		WITHDRAWAL		BALANCE	

FORM 7

INDIVIDUAL ACCOUNT PAGE

			$			$		
	ACCOUNT CATEGORY		ALLOCATION			ALLOCATION		
DATE	TRANSACTION		DEPOSIT		WITHDRAWAL		BALANCE	

FORM 7

INDIVIDUAL ACCOUNT PAGE

	ACCOUNT CATEGORY	$ _____ ALLOCATION	$ _____ ALLOCATION

DATE	TRANSACTION	DEPOSIT		WITHDRAWAL		BALANCE	

INDIVIDUAL ACCOUNT PAGE

ACCOUNT CATEGORY		$ ALLOCATION		$ ALLOCATION	

DATE	TRANSACTION	DEPOSIT		WITHDRAWAL		BALANCE	

FORM 7

INDIVIDUAL ACCOUNT PAGE

$ _____ $ _____

ACCOUNT CATEGORY   **ALLOCATION**   **ALLOCATION**

DATE	TRANSACTION	DEPOSIT		WITHDRAWAL		BALANCE	

FORM 7

INDIVIDUAL ACCOUNT PAGE

| | ACCOUNT CATEGORY | $ | | | $ | |
| | | ALLOCATION | | | ALLOCATION | |

DATE	TRANSACTION	DEPOSIT		WITHDRAWAL		BALANCE	

INDIVIDUAL ACCOUNT PAGE

| | | $ _____ | | $ _____ |
| ACCOUNT CATEGORY | | ALLOCATION | | ALLOCATION |

DATE	TRANSACTION	DEPOSIT		WITHDRAWAL		BALANCE	

FORM 7

INDIVIDUAL ACCOUNT PAGE

				$			
	ACCOUNT CATEGORY			ALLOCATION		ALLOCATION	

DATE	TRANSACTION	DEPOSIT		WITHDRAWAL		BALANCE	

FORM 7

INDIVIDUAL ACCOUNT PAGE

ACCOUNT CATEGORY		$ _____ ALLOCATION		$ _____ ALLOCATION	

DATE	TRANSACTION	DEPOSIT	WITHDRAWAL	BALANCE	

FORM 7

INDIVIDUAL ACCOUNT PAGE

ACCOUNT CATEGORY		$ ALLOCATION		$ ALLOCATION
DATE	**TRANSACTION**	**DEPOSIT**	**WITHDRAWAL**	**BALANCE**

FORM 7

INDIVIDUAL ACCOUNT PAGE

		$ _____		$ _____	
	ACCOUNT CATEGORY	ALLOCATION		ALLOCATION	
DATE	TRANSACTION	DEPOSIT	WITHDRAWAL	BALANCE	

FORM 7

INDIVIDUAL ACCOUNT PAGE

_____ $ _____ $ _____
ACCOUNT CATEGORY   ALLOCATION   ALLOCATION

DATE	TRANSACTION	DEPOSIT		WITHDRAWAL		BALANCE	

INDIVIDUAL ACCOUNT PAGE

		$		$	
	ACCOUNT CATEGORY	ALLOCATION		ALLOCATION	
DATE	TRANSACTION	DEPOSIT	WITHDRAWAL	BALANCE	

INDIVIDUAL ACCOUNT PAGE

	ACCOUNT CATEGORY	$ ALLOCATION		$ ALLOCATION

DATE	TRANSACTION	DEPOSIT	WITHDRAWAL	BALANCE

INDIVIDUAL ACCOUNT PAGE

ACCOUNT CATEGORY		$ ALLOCATION		$ ALLOCATION

DATE	TRANSACTION	DEPOSIT	WITHDRAWAL	BALANCE

INDIVIDUAL ACCOUNT PAGE

		$		$
	ACCOUNT CATEGORY	ALLOCATION		ALLOCATION

DATE	TRANSACTION	DEPOSIT		WITHDRAWAL		BALANCE	

FORM 7

CHECKBOOK LEDGER

DATE	CK.#	TRANSACTION		DEPOSIT		WITHDRAWAL		BALANCE	
			○						
			○						
			○						
			○						
			○						
			○						
			○						
			○						
			○						
			○						
			○						
			○						
			○						
			○						
			○						
			○						
			○						
			○						
			○						
			○						
			○						
			○						
			○						
			○						
			○						
			○						
			○						
			○						
			○						
			○						
			○						
			○						
			○						

FORM 7A

CHECKBOOK LEDGER

DATE	CK.#	TRANSACTION	DEPOSIT	WITHDRAWAL	BALANCE

FORM 7A

CHECKBOOK LEDGER

DATE	CK.#	TRANSACTION	DEPOSIT		WITHDRAWAL		BALANCE	
		○						
		○						
		○						
		○						
		○						
		○						
		○						
		○						
		○						
		○						
		○						
		○						
		○						
		○						
		○						
		○						
		○						
		○						
		○						
		○						
		○						
		○						
		○						
		○						
		○						
		○						
		○						
		○						
		○						
		○						
		○						
		○						

FORM 7A

CHECKBOOK LEDGER

DATE	CK.#	TRANSACTION	DEPOSIT	WITHDRAWAL	BALANCE
		○			
		○			
		○			
		○			
		○			
		○			
		○			
		○			
		○			
		○			
		○			
		○			
		○			
		○			
		○			
		○			
		○			
		○			
		○			
		○			
		○			
		○			
		○			
		○			
		○			
		○			
		○			
		○			
		○			
		○			
		○			
		○			

FORM 7A

CHECKBOOK LEDGER

DATE	CK.#	TRANSACTION	DEPOSIT		WITHDRAWAL		BALANCE	
		○						
		○						
		○						
		○						
		○						
		○						
		○						
		○						
		○						
		○						
		○						
		○						
		○						
		○						
		○						
		○						
		○						
		○						
		○						
		○						
		○						
		○						
		○						
		○						
		○						
		○						
		○						
		○						
		○						
		○						
		○						
		○						
		○						

FORM 7A

CHECKBOOK LEDGER

DATE	CK.#	TRANSACTION		DEPOSIT		WITHDRAWAL		BALANCE	
			◯						
			◯						
			◯						
			◯						
			◯						
			◯						
			◯						
			◯						
			◯						
			◯						
			◯						
			◯						
			◯						
			◯						
			◯						
			◯						
			◯						
			◯						
			◯						
			◯						
			◯						
			◯						
			◯						
			◯						
			◯						
			◯						
			◯						
			◯						
			◯						
			◯						
			◯						
			◯						
			◯						
			◯						

FORM 7A

CHECKBOOK LEDGER

DATE	CK.#	TRANSACTION		DEPOSIT		WITHDRAWAL		BALANCE	
			○						
			○						
			○						
			○						
			○						
			○						
			○						
			○						
			○						
			○						
			○						
			○						
			○						
			○						
			○						
			○						
			○						
			○						
			○						
			○						
			○						
			○						
			○						
			○						
			○						
			○						
			○						
			○						
			○						
			○						
			○						

FORM 7A

CHECKBOOK LEDGER

DATE	CK.#	TRANSACTION	DEPOSIT		WITHDRAWAL		BALANCE	
		○						
		○						
		○						
		○						
		○						
		○						
		○						
		○						
		○						
		○						
		○						
		○						
		○						
		○						
		○						
		○						
		○						
		○						
		○						
		○						
		○						
		○						
		○						
		○						
		○						
		○						
		○						
		○						
		○						
		○						
		○						
		○						
		○						

FORM 7A

CHECKBOOK LEDGER

DATE	CK.#	TRANSACTION		DEPOSIT		WITHDRAWAL		BALANCE	
			○						
			○						
			○						
			○						
			○						
			○						
			○						
			○						
			○						
			○						
			○						
			○						
			○						
			○						
			○						
			○						
			○						
			○						
			○						
			○						
			○						
			○						
			○						
			○						
			○						
			○						
			○						
			○						
			○						
			○						
			○						

FORM 7A

CHECKBOOK LEDGER

DATE	CK.#	TRANSACTION		DEPOSIT		WITHDRAWAL		BALANCE	
			○						
			○						
			○						
			○						
			○						
			○						
			○						
			○						
			○						
			○						
			○						
			○						
			○						
			○						
			○						
			○						
			○						
			○						
			○						
			○						
			○						
			○						
			○						
			○						
			○						
			○						
			○						
			○						
			○						
			○						
			○						
			○						
			○						
			○						

FORM 7A

CHECKBOOK LEDGER

DATE	CK.#	TRANSACTION	DEPOSIT	WITHDRAWAL	BALANCE
		○			
		○			
		○			
		○			
		○			
		○			
		○			
		○			
		○			
		○			
		○			
		○			
		○			
		○			
		○			
		○			
		○			
		○			
		○			
		○			
		○			
		○			
		○			
		○			
		○			
		○			
		○			
		○			
		○			
		○			
		○			
		○			

FORM 7A

CHECKBOOK LEDGER

DATE	CK.#	TRANSACTION		DEPOSIT		WITHDRAWAL		BALANCE	
			○						
			○						
			○						
			○						
			○						
			○						
			○						
			○						
			○						
			○						
			○						
			○						
			○						
			○						
			○						
			○						
			○						
			○						
			○						
			○						
			○						
			○						
			○						
			○						
			○						
			○						
			○						
			○						
			○						
			○						
			○						
			○						
			○						

FORM 7A

CHECKBOOK LEDGER

DATE	CK.#	TRANSACTION		DEPOSIT		WITHDRAWAL		BALANCE	
			○						
			○						
			○						
			○						
			○						
			○						
			○						
			○						
			○						
			○						
			○						
			○						
			○						
			○						
			○						
			○						
			○						
			○						
			○						
			○						
			○						
			○						
			○						
			○						
			○						
			○						
			○						
			○						
			○						
			○						
			○						
			○						
			○						
			○						

FORM 7A

CHECKBOOK LEDGER

DATE	CK.#	TRANSACTION	DEPOSIT		WITHDRAWAL		BALANCE	
		◯						
		◯						
		◯						
		◯						
		◯						
		◯						
		◯						
		◯						
		◯						
		◯						
		◯						
		◯						
		◯						
		◯						
		◯						
		◯						
		◯						
		◯						
		◯						
		◯						
		◯						
		◯						
		◯						
		◯						
		◯						
		◯						
		◯						
		◯						
		◯						
		◯						
		◯						
		◯						
		◯						
		◯						
		◯						
		◯						

FORM 7A

CHECKBOOK LEDGER

DATE	CK.#	TRANSACTION		DEPOSIT		WITHDRAWAL		BALANCE	
			○						
			○						
			○						
			○						
			○						
			○						
			○						
			○						
			○						
			○						
			○						
			○						
			○						
			○						
			○						
			○						
			○						
			○						
			○						
			○						
			○						
			○						
			○						
			○						
			○						
			○						
			○						
			○						
			○						
			○						
			○						

FORM 7A

CHECKBOOK LEDGER

DATE	CK.#	TRANSACTION		DEPOSIT		WITHDRAWAL		BALANCE	
			○						
			○						
			○						
			○						
			○						
			○						
			○						
			○						
			○						
			○						
			○						
			○						
			○						
			○						
			○						
			○						
			○						
			○						
			○						
			○						
			○						
			○						
			○						
			○						
			○						
			○						
			○						
			○						
			○						
			○						
			○						
			○						
			○						
			○						

FORM 7A

CHECKBOOK LEDGER

DATE	CK.#	TRANSACTION	DEPOSIT		WITHDRAWAL		BALANCE	
		◯						
		◯						
		◯						
		◯						
		◯						
		◯						
		◯						
		◯						
		◯						
		◯						
		◯						
		◯						
		◯						
		◯						
		◯						
		◯						
		◯						
		◯						
		◯						
		◯						
		◯						
		◯						
		◯						
		◯						
		◯						
		◯						
		◯						
		◯						
		◯						
		◯						
		◯						
		◯						

FORM 7A

CHECKBOOK LEDGER

DATE	CK.#	TRANSACTION		DEPOSIT		WITHDRAWAL		BALANCE	
			◯						
			◯						
			◯						
			◯						
			◯						
			◯						
			◯						
			◯						
			◯						
			◯						
			◯						
			◯						
			◯						
			◯						
			◯						
			◯						
			◯						
			◯						
			◯						
			◯						
			◯						
			◯						
			◯						
			◯						
			◯						
			◯						
			◯						
			◯						
			◯						
			◯						
			◯						
			◯						
			◯						

FORM 7A

LIST OF DEBTS
as of_____

TO WHOM OWED	CONTACT NAME / PHONE NUMBER	PAYOFF AMOUNT	PAYMENTS LEFT	MONTHLY PAYMENT	DUE DATE

FORM 8

LIST OF DEBTS
as of_____

TO WHOM OWED	CONTACT NAME PHONE NUMBER	PAYOFF AMOUNT	PAYMENTS LEFT	MONTHLY PAYMENT	DUE DATE

FORM 8

LIST OF DEBTS
as of_____

TO WHOM OWED	CONTACT NAME PHONE NUMBER	PAYOFF AMOUNT	PAYMENTS LEFT	MONTHLY PAYMENT	DUE DATE

FORM 8

LIST OF DEBTS
as of_____

TO WHOM OWED	CONTACT NAME PHONE NUMBER	PAYOFF AMOUNT	PAYMENTS LEFT	MONTHLY PAYMENT	DUE DATE

FORM 8

IMPULSE LIST

DATE	IMPULSE ITEM	1	2	3

FORM 8A

IMPULSE LIST

DATE	IMPULSE ITEM	1	2	3

FORM 8A

INDIVIDUAL ACCOUNT PAGE

	ACCOUNT CATEGORY	$ ALLOCATION		$ ALLOCATION

DATE	TRANSACTION	DEPOSIT		WITHDRAWAL		BALANCE	

FORM 7

CHECKBOOK LEDGER

DATE	CK.#	TRANSACTION	DEPOSIT		WITHDRAWAL		BALANCE	
		◯						
		◯						
		◯						
		◯						
		◯						
		◯						
		◯						
		◯						
		◯						
		◯						
		◯						
		◯						
		◯						
		◯						
		◯						
		◯						
		◯						
		◯						
		◯						
		◯						
		◯						
		◯						
		◯						
		◯						
		◯						
		◯						
		◯						
		◯						
		◯						
		◯						
		◯						
		◯						
		◯						
		◯						

FORM 7A